Beginning the Walk

JESUS
THE WAY

Ron and Mary Bennett

For a free catalog
of NavPress books & Bible studies call
1-800-366-7788 (USA) or 1-800-839-4769 (Canada).

www.NavPress.com

The Navigators is an international Christian organization. Our mission is to reach, disciple, and equip people to know Christ and to make Him known through successive generations. We envision multitudes of diverse people in the United States and every other nation who have a passionate love for Christ, live a lifestyle of sharing Christ's love, and multiply spiritual laborers among those without Christ.

NavPress is the publishing ministry of The Navigators. NavPress publications help believers learn biblical truth and apply what they learn to their lives and ministries. Our mission is to stimulate spiritual formation among our readers.

The Navigators' Church Discipleship Ministry (CDM) is focused on helping churches become more intentional in disciplemaking. CDM staff nationwide are available to help church leadership develop the critical components that will enable them to accomplish Christ's Great Commission. For further information on how CDM can help you, contact our office at 719-594-2446.

© 2004 by The Navigators' Church Discipleship Ministry, Inc.

www.navigators.org/cdm

NAVPRESS and the NAVPRESS logo are registered trademarks of NavPress. Absence of ® in connection with marks of NavPress or other parties does not indicate an absence of registration of those marks.

ISBN 13: 978-1-57683-349-0
ISBN 10: 1-57683-349-6

Cover design by Arvid Wallen
Cover imagery by Arvid Wallen
Creative Team: Bob Walz, Steve Parolini, Arvid Wallen, Kathy Mosier, Glynese Northam, Pat Reinheimer

Some of the anecdotal illustrations in this book are true to life and are included with the permission of the persons involved. All other illustrations are composites of real situations, and any resemblance to people living or dead is coincidental.

Printed in the United States of America

3 4 5 6 7 8 9 10 / 11 10 09 08 07

For further information regarding this material and other discipling resources contact:

The Navigators
P.O. Box 6000
Colorado Springs, CO 80934

About Beginning the Walk

This study is part of a three-book series called *Beginning the Walk*. These studies are designed to help believers begin their new life with Christ. Although intended for individual use, they can also be used with a mentor or in a small group. However you use this series, you won't need an extensive church or religious background to get started. Each study begins right where you are — with the basics. The series includes the following three studies:

- *Jesus: The Way*
- *Jesus: The Truth*
- *Jesus: The Life*

We recommend you begin with the book you are now holding: *Jesus: The Way*. Each study contains six lessons with a key Scripture verse at the beginning of each lesson. A lesson will probably take thirty to forty-five minutes to complete, but don't feel bound by that time frame. If you get through them faster, that's okay. And if you spend more time in each lesson, that's okay too.

The Bible passages used in this series are included in the text of the lessons. Still, we highly recommend you have a personal Bible as well. In addition to reading the Scripture in the lesson, you may want to look up the references and read them in your own Bible. This will broaden your understanding as you discover more about the context of the Scripture passages.

Contents

Through faith we have a new relationship with God that is reflected in each person of the Trinity: Father, Son, and Holy Spirit. The journey you are beginning is based on a personal, dynamic relationship with God as expressed in each person of the Trinity.

In Christ we are a brand-new creation. God has changed our essential being. He not only has forgiven us but also has given us a brand-new identity.

Christ is the center around which we find our place. He is the explanation of the invisible God, and He is the gracious leader for those who choose to follow.

Christ is now our constant companion. He walks beside us, lives within us, and goes before us. He knows the path, the destination, and all the hazards ahead.

As we travel the journey with Christ, we will become like Him. We will reflect His nature and character. God has a new wardrobe for us that reflects our new nature.

We are created and called to God's purposes. His plans go beyond this life into eternity. We are made by God and for God. Discovering His will for us is a treasure of great value.

Preface

Therefore as you have received Christ Jesus the Lord, so walk in Him.
COLOSSIANS 2:6, NASB

Welcome to an incredible journey called "your new life in Christ." When you came to a personal faith in Christ, you began a lifelong journey that you will complete only when you see Jesus face-to-face. He made this claim and promise in John 10:10: "I came so they can have real and eternal life, more and better life than they ever dreamed of."

Whenever the Bible talks about new life (or as *The Message* puts it, "more and better life"), it is talking about more than just new habits or patterns for daily living. The life that results from faith in Christ is life with a new spiritual dimension. It is a relational journey that has adventure, excitement, and purpose. The Bible uses the term *eternal life* to describe this new reality. Jesus explained it like this in John 17:3: "And this is the real and eternal life: that they know you, the one and only true God, and Jesus Christ, whom you sent."

Life, in the language of the Bible, is not a single event. It is a journey of knowing Christ, experiencing the reality of His presence in your life, and discovering more of who He is as you walk through each day. This life has both quality and quantity. In terms of quality, God gives meaning and purpose to the practical experiences of life. In terms of quantity, this relationship with Christ lasts from the moment of your faith discovery until . . . forever.

Jesus Christ is the central focus of this life. As you become more familiar with the Bible, you will discover how important Jesus really is. Most of us have developed a working concept of God based on our past experiences. For some, God is a distant landlord; to others, He is a vigilant policeman. Still others see God as an impersonal force or a cosmic Santa Claus. Jesus Christ came into our world to reveal the true nature and person of God. He came to correct and clarify our understanding of God. To know Christ is to discover God, as we see in Hebrews 1:1-3:

> Going through a long line of prophets, God has been addressing our ancestors in different ways for centuries. Recently he spoke to us directly through his Son. By his Son, God created the world in the beginning, and it will all belong to the Son at the end. This Son perfectly mirrors God, and is stamped with God's nature. He holds everything together by what he says — powerful words!

The journey of knowing Christ is more than gathering information, yet it needs to be grounded in truth. This journey is more than an emotional event, yet it contains many significant experiences. This relational journey touches every part of who we are. It affects our mind, emotions, and will. It works from the inside out and the outside in. It is personal. It is private and public. It is visible and invisible, simple and complex. It is incomprehensible yet understandable. It is beyond our experience yet touches everything about us that is real.

God is the designer and author of life, so understanding who He is will help you appreciate the gift of life He has given you. *Beginning the Walk* will move you along on your journey of knowing and experiencing Christ personally.

As you begin your journey, you may wish you had maps or blueprints to show you where to go or what to do. This study series can help. Some of the concepts introduced in these pages may be totally new for you, and some may be familiar. Some may challenge what you previously thought, and others may even be confusing. Remember that this is a lifelong journey — a journey that will take you into new discoveries and experiences. Clarity will come as you continue on the journey.

The Bible is our primary source for truth on this journey. Written over the course of 1,500 years by various authors who were inspired by God, the Bible includes a number of literary styles. Some of it is written as history, some as poetry. Some of the books are letters to individuals; others are letters to groups of people. The Bible claims to be the revelation of God to man, God's own story line with man. By studying the Bible, we can move beyond the general revelation of God that we see in nature to discover His character, heart, and purposes.

In the past, you may have found the Bible boring, baffling, or bewildering. Now, however, as you begin your relational journey with Christ, the Bible will come alive. As you read the Bible, you will begin to understand what it means to have a new life in Christ.

The Bible will be your best resource for the journey. But like any journey, there will be times when you feel lost or unsure about which path to take. That's because a life of faith prompts just as many questions as answers.

A few years ago, an airline company offered mystery trips. People bought tickets and showed up at the airport with bags packed for a three-day journey. All arrangements were made for a surprise weekend in a major city in the United States, but ticket holders wouldn't know which one until they got on the plane. The mystery added a sense of adventure to an otherwise familiar activity.

But what if, instead of U.S. cities, the plane whisked you off to a mystery location unlike anything you had ever known? One where *everything* seemed new and unfamiliar. One where the culture, the government, the language, the currency, even the landscape was foreign.

When you came to personal faith in Jesus Christ, you were given a ticket for this kind of mystery trip. And now that the plane has landed, you have stepped into a place called the kingdom of God. While you will probably have lots of questions about this place, you will soon discover that the kingdom of God promises real-life adventure in the "now" as well as an incomprehensibly exciting "not yet" called heaven. You will learn that living in the kingdom of God brings new freedoms and new relationships; that it results in a new perspective, purpose, and direction; and that it gives you new resources and responsibilities.

Teaching you how to relate to Jesus Christ and to live successfully in the "now" aspect of the kingdom is the purpose of this study (and of the others in the *Beginning the Walk* series). Regardless of your religious (or nonreligious) background, these lessons will help you understand more about the exciting journey you began by putting your faith in Christ.

The apostle Paul said that new life in Christ brings about significant changes. In 2 Corinthians 5:17, he wrote to the new believers in Corinth, "Therefore if anyone is in Christ, he is a new creature; the old things passed away; behold, new things have come" (NASB). As you begin to understand these changes, you will be better able to participate in your new life adventure. You will be able to fully utilize the resources and enjoy all the benefits of life in the kingdom of God.

Enjoy the journey!

Acknowledgment

We want to express our appreciation to Bob Walz for his outstanding coaching and invaluable advice in the development of this material. His insight and encouragement were a constant source of energy and motivation.

Introduction

*For there is a hope to attain a journey's end when there is a
path which stretches between the traveler and his goal. But if there is no path,
or if a man does not know which way to go, there is little use in knowing the
destination. As it is, there is one road, and one only. Well secured against the
possibility of going astray; and this road is provided by one who is himself
both God and man. As God, he is the goal; as man, he is the way.*

SAINT AUGUSTINE, *CONFESSIONS*

*Y*ou may have come to faith in Jesus Christ at a very identifiable moment in your life or through a process that is less definable. You may have endured significant crises that propelled you along in your search for God, or your story may be one of a quiet inner heart tug. Regardless of the path you took to Christ, those steps were only the beginning.

Christianity was initially called "The Way." Followers of Christ were identified with a way of life Jesus demonstrated and taught. Jesus even referred to Himself as "the way" in John 14:6: "I am the way, and the truth, and the life" (NASB).

Walking with Jesus Christ on this journey will bring both internal and external changes. Some changes will happen quickly, while others will take years. The apostle Paul referred to things being "new" for those in Christ. As we journey on with Christ, our behavior changes, our thinking changes, even our desires and values change. Life really does become new.

For any journey to be successful, you have to first prepare. This includes knowing where you are going and how you are going to get there. To help you prepare for your faith journey, this study will introduce basic concepts that can help you avoid painful detours and roadblocks.

These concepts are themes taught throughout the Bible. We have chosen to focus primarily on two books in the New Testament: Ephesians and Colossians, two letters written by the apostle Paul during his ministry in the first century. They were written to groups of new believers in Christ who were beginning their own journeys.

These are the concepts you'll explore in *Jesus: The Way*:

- Your New Connection in Christ
- Your New Creation in Christ
- Your New Center in Christ
- Your New Companionship in Christ
- Your New Clothes in Christ
- Your New Calling in Christ

New Connection

NEXT STEPS

Your journey with Christ involves a new relationship with God: a personal connection. Faith in Christ breaks down the barrier separating us from God and gives us access to a deep, personal friendship with the eternal God.

Now God has us where he wants us, with all the time in this world and the next to shower grace and kindness upon us in Christ Jesus.

EPHESIANS 2:7

While in the army's Infantry Officer Candidate School in 1968, I was part of a military honor guard that welcomed the president of the United States to our military base. He walked by so close to me that I could have reached out and touched him. For a brief moment I caught his eye. That is a far cry from having a personal friendship with the president, but it's the closest I've been to a powerful leader. It seems as if the more powerful a leader is, the more distant and unapproachable he or she becomes to ordinary people.

What a contrast this is to the approachability of Jesus! The awesome Creator of the universe planned long ago to relate to each person "up close and personal." Jesus' role in history made that possible. Regardless of your past, God wants a personal relationship with you.

There are two key aspects of any relationship: honest dialogue and shared experiences. Both are essential. Dialogue without mutual experiences leaves you intellectually stimulated but relationally challenged. Shared experiences can be enjoyable, but without dialogue they remain shallow and incomplete. Relating to Christ works in much the same way. He wants both your dialogue and your experiences.

So who is this God who wants a relationship with you? The Bible begins with the words, "In the beginning God . . ." (NASB). The Bible doesn't set out to prove God but rather reveals Him. In the Old Testament, God is described using various names such as *the powerful God*, *the holy God*, and *the mighty God*. Unlike most other religions, the God of the Bible is not just the supreme God; He is the one and only God. The Bible also shows God as having three personalities or distinct persons. This concept is called the Trinity or Tri-unity.

Trinity is a word not found in Scripture, but it is used to express the doctrine of the unity of God as subsisting in three distinct persons. The propositions involved in the doctrine are these:

1. That God is one, and that there is but one God.

2. That the Father is a divine person, distinct from the Son and the Holy Spirit.

3. That Jesus Christ is truly God and yet is a person distinct from the Father and the Holy Spirit.

4. That the Holy Spirit is also a distinct, divine person.[*]

When people relate to God, they relate both to God as "one" and to God as expressed in each person of the Trinity. This becomes more evident in the New Testament, where the persons of the Trinity are referred to more directly in their unique roles. Jesus is often referred to as the second person of the Trinity, God the Son, and is the focal point of the Gospels, the first four books of the New Testament. The Holy Spirit, referred to as the third person of the Trinity, is the focal point of the book of Acts. When the apostle Paul and the other writers wrote to the early churches, they used the term *God*, referring to the first person of the Trinity, or God the Father.

Let's look at how each person of the Trinity is involved in the new connection you have with God.

---

[*]M. G. Easton, MA, DD, *Illustrated Bible Dictionary*, 3rd ed. (Nashville: Nelson, 1897), NavPress software, 1996.

LOVED BY THE FATHER

In stark contrast to the pagan gods or the sketches of God as expressed in various other religions, our God is revealed not only as powerful and holy, but as intimately loving. The apostle Paul described God in Ephesians 1:3-6:

> How blessed is God! And what a blessing he is! He's the Father of our Master, Jesus Christ, and takes us to the high places of blessing in him. Long before he laid down earth's foundations, he had us in mind, had settled on us as the focus of his love, to be made whole and holy by his love. Long, long ago he decided to adopt us into his family through Jesus Christ. (What pleasure he took in planning this!) He wanted us to enter into the celebration of his lavish gift-giving by the hand of his beloved Son.

Q1. What do you discover about God from these verses?

Q2. What does it mean to you when someone or something is the "focus of his love"?

Q3. Which of these statements have you thought or believed?

_____ I am too insignificant to be important to God.
_____ I have too much baggage in my life to ever receive God's love.
_____ I don't deserve God's love, so I can't accept it.
_____ God is too distant for someone to relate to on a personal level.

Q4. What does this passage say about your value to God?

One way the apostle Paul described your new relationship with God was by the term *adoption*. In Paul's culture, people were adopted when there was no natural, legal heir. Adoption gave the individual the permanent legal name and all the privileges of a natural son or daughter.

The apostle John referred to the same idea in John 1:12: "Yet to all who received him [Jesus Christ], to those who believed in his name, he gave the right to become children of God" (NIV).

FREED BY THE SON

Freedom, in part, comes as you are released from your past guilt and separation from God and brought into a personal and vital relationship with Christ. A fish tossed up on the banks of a river is initially very active but not free. Placed back into the water, the fish is truly free. Living without faith in God is like being a fish on the bank. You may be frantically active, but you are doomed. Freedom comes as you are placed into the environment you were designed for, the safe and secure love of God.

To experience your freedom, you must understand two foundational truths regarding your new connection. One is that you are "in Christ," and the second is that Christ is "in you." They are like opposite sides of the same coin, linked together to form the whole. Part of the miracle of experiencing Christ is that both of these truths became a reality the moment you came to faith in Christ. However, it is a lifelong journey to understand and work out the implications of these two truths.

Being "in Christ" means that you now share His identity. It means that God sees you just like He sees Jesus. As Jesus is God's Son, you are also now one of His children. Because Jesus is accepted before God, you also are accepted with your sins forgiven.

Christ "in you" means that Christ makes your heart His dwelling place. In the Old Testament, God's presence was in the Hebrew tabernacle (or temple) in a place called the Holy of Holies. Since the death and resurrection of Jesus Christ, God now lives in the hearts of His people. The apostle Paul explained it as follows in Ephesians 1:7-12:

> Because of the sacrifice of the Messiah, his blood poured out on the altar of the Cross, we're a free people — free of penalties and punishments chalked up by all our misdeeds. And not just barely free, either. *Abundantly* free! He thought of everything, provided for everything we could possibly need, letting

us in on the plans he took such delight in making. He set it all out before us in Christ, a long-range plan in which everything would be brought together and summed up in him, everything in deepest heaven, everything on planet earth. It's in Christ that we find out who we are and what we are living for. Long before we first heard of Christ and got our hopes up, he had his eye on us, had designs on us for glorious living, part of the overall purpose he is working out in everything and everyone.

Q5. As described in the passage above, what was accomplished by Christ's sacrifice for you on the cross?

Misdeeds or *sins* mean missing the mark of God's moral standard. They refer to both the inward state of your heart and your outward behavior.

Q6. Look again at Ephesians 1:7-12. What are the benefits of being "in Christ"?

Both your identity and your destiny are wrapped up in your relationship with Christ. Discovering who Christ is and what He is doing is key to knowing how you should live. He desires to bring you alongside Him and make your life work. Jesus said in Matthew 11:28-30:

"Are you tired? Worn out? Burned out on religion? Come to me. Get away with me and you'll recover your life. I'll show you how to take a real rest. Walk with me and work with me — watch how I do it. Learn the unforced rhythms of

> grace. I won't lay anything heavy or ill-fitting on you. Keep company with me and you'll learn to live freely and lightly."

CERTIFIED BY THE HOLY SPIRIT

The role of the Holy Spirit, the third person of the Trinity, took on a new significance after Christ was crucified, rose again, and ascended into heaven. Jesus told His disciples to get ready because things were going to be different. No longer was God simply going to be present alongside them, but He was actually going to live *in* each person of faith. The Holy Spirit is also God's seal of certification in your life that you are officially His. The apostle Paul said the following in Ephesians 1:13-14:

> It's in Christ that you, once you heard the truth and believed it (this Message of your salvation), found yourselves home free — signed, sealed, and delivered by the Holy Spirit. This signet from God is the first installment on what's coming, a reminder that we'll get everything God has planned for us, a praising and glorious life.

God has not only forgiven you; He actually lives in you. The Holy Spirit's presence in your life is a seal (signet) of that truth. Just as a king's seal was the official stamp of authenticity, the Holy Spirit is your seal giving authenticity to your new connection with God. This may not seem real to you now, but it is true nonetheless. You will learn as you walk with Christ how to recognize the reality of God's Spirit within you.

Q7. What did you learn about the Holy Spirit from this passage in Ephesians?

One of the things the Holy Spirit does is help you understand who God is and who you are. He works quietly in your inner person to bring clarity and awareness. The apostle Paul described it as follows in Romans 8:16: "God's Spirit touches our spirits and confirms who we really are. We know who he is, and we know who we are: Father and children."

The Holy Spirit's presence also serves as a reminder that there is more to come. God has an inheritance for you that is a future reality. We can apply to ourselves what Jesus reminded the disciples just before He was to leave them to take His place in heaven:

> "Don't let this throw you. You trust God, don't you? Trust me. There is plenty of room for you in my Father's home. If that weren't so, would I have told you that I'm on my way to get a room ready for you? And if I'm on my way to get your room ready, I'll come back and get you so you can live where I live." (John 14:1-3)

Q8. What do these verses promise you as a member of God's family?

SUMMARY

Through faith we have a new relationship with God that is reflected in each person of the Trinity: Father, Son, and Holy Spirit. Our journey is based on a personal, dynamic relationship with God as expressed in each person of the Trinity:

- Loved by the Father
- Freed by the Son
- Certified by the Holy Spirit

PRAYER

Thank You, God, for making it possible for me to relate to You personally. I realize that I have no merit of my own that would earn me the right to come into Your presence. As Your adopted child, I want to know You more and learn how to live as a member of Your family. Open my mind and change my heart so I would know the joy of a deep friendship with You.

LESSON 2

New Creation

NEXT STEPS

Your journey with Christ begins with God giving you a new nature. We are new creations. We may look the same on the outside, but something inside has changed dramatically. We are now in Christ, and Christ is in us. This results in a new identity.

Now we look inside, and what we see is that anyone united with the Messiah gets a fresh start, is created new. The old life is gone; a new life burgeons! Look at it!
2 CORINTHIANS 5:17

Early in the cold war, a Russian pilot flew his MiG fighter plane to Japan and asked for asylum in the United States. After the predictable flurry of excitement over having a state-of-the-art Russian plane to analyze, government officials debriefed the pilot and eventually brought him to the United States where he was given a new identity and citizenship. He was instructed in the beliefs and systems of his new country and given financial resources to get started in his new life.

Interviewed years later, the pilot reflected on how difficult it initially was living with his new identity. He had been told he was free, yet he imagined the KGB or the U.S. equivalent was shadowing his every move. He had the freedom to travel anywhere he wanted but still felt as if he needed to ask permission. At times he experienced an unexplainable urge to go back to the life he had willingly left — to go back to the "known"—even though that meant certain death.

You are probably experiencing similar adjustment challenges. It takes time for your perspective, values, and behavior to change, yet faith in Christ instantly changes your standing with God. Your position with God is not based on how you feel or even act. It is based on what Christ has done for you at the cross. Too often new believers base their standing with God on how

20

they feel at the moment or on their behavior. Don't make this mistake. Base your standing with God on what He has said is true about you.

You Are Alive

The Bible describes our life outside of a relationship with Christ as being "dead." We are cut off or separated from a vital and personal connection with God and His Spirit. But when we accept Christ by faith, we are made "alive." The apostle Paul wrote in Ephesians 2:1-6:

> It wasn't so long ago that you were mired in that old stagnant life of sin. You let the world, which doesn't know the first thing about living, tell you how to live. You filled your lungs with polluted unbelief, and then exhaled disobedience. We all did it, all of us doing what we felt like doing, when we felt like doing it, all of us in the same boat. It's a wonder God didn't lose his temper and do away with the whole lot of us. Instead, immense in mercy and with an incredible love, he embraced us. He took our sin-dead lives and made us alive in Christ. He did all this on his own, with no help from us! Then he picked us up and set us down in highest heaven in company with Jesus, our Messiah.

Q1. How did Paul describe life before coming to faith in Christ?

Q2. What did God do for you?

Q3. Why did He do it?

> *Mercy* means not getting what we deserve: God's wrath;
> *love* or *grace* means getting the undeserved goodness of God.

Becoming alive implies that we were previously dead. In Genesis 3, we read the story of how, through Adam and Eve, humanity became spiritually dead. You may not have thought of yourself as dead, but that is how God describes a person without Christ. This concept is repeated throughout Scripture. It graphically illustrates the sorry state of life without God and the dramatic change that takes place when one comes to Christ by faith. Being dead like this explains a lot about your past. Being made alive implies a lot about your future.

This new aliveness may manifest itself in various ways in your life. Some notice it as an appetite for the Bible, the Word of God. Others discover it in the peace they find or in their freedom from guilt. It may start as a seed of awareness and grow. Regardless of how you feel, God has given you new life. Believe it and watch how it displays itself day by day.

YOU ARE A SAINT

The apostle Paul began most of his letters to the early churches with the greeting, "To the saints." Saints! When you read the letters and learn about some of the issues and problems those new believers were having, you might question Paul's greeting. The word *saint* means morally blameless, "called-out one," or "set-apart one." Another word for it is *holy*.

God's declaration of our holiness is not a response to our perfection. God calls us holy because He no longer sees us on the basis of our own merit (how good or how sinful we are) but through the perfection of His Son. You are no longer referred to as a sinner who is separate from God but as a saint who still sins. God has established your core identity as that of a saint. Your journey involves learning how to live as a saint, or a "set-apart one." The apostle Paul said it this way in Colossians 1:21-22:

> You yourselves are a case study of what he does. At one time you all had your backs turned to God, thinking rebellious thoughts of him, giving him trouble every chance you got. But now, by giving himself completely at the Cross, actually *dying* for you, Christ brought you over to God's side and put your lives together, whole and holy in his presence.

Q4. In the previous passage, circle the things that are true about you now.

Q5. What do you think it means to be "brought over to God's side"?

YOU ARE FORGIVEN

Another part of your new identity is that you are forgiven. God did not ignore your sin but in fact dealt with it through Jesus' sacrifice on the cross. Forgiveness was not free. Christ did what we could not do on our own.

Throughout the Old Testament as God related to the nation of Israel, He established an elaborate system of sacrifices that dealt with the issue of sin. Much of the symbolism of that system is lost in our culture, but there is no doubt that God takes sin seriously. Sin offends His very nature. The beauty of Jesus' sacrifice is that through it, God's character is revealed in wonderful fullness — including both His love and justice. The apostle Paul said in Colossians 2:13-14:

> When you were stuck in your old sin-dead life, you were incapable of responding to God. God brought you alive — right along with Christ! Think of it! All sins forgiven, the slate wiped clean, that old arrest warrant canceled and nailed to Christ's Cross.

Q6. What do these verses say God has done for you in Christ?

Q7. Since these things are true, how should you respond?

YOU ARE A CITIZEN

The apostle Paul talked about this new journey of faith as life in a new country or kingdom. This word picture helps us see who we are in light of both Christ (the King of the kingdom) and our fellow travelers. During His ministry, Christ talked a great deal about the kingdom of God. The concept of a kingdom isn't particularly relevant in modern society. We have to look back to medieval times or perhaps to the images in Tolkien's *Lord of the Rings* to find a kingdom reference point. Yet the kingdom of God is not a geographic place with castles, kings, or moats. Paul referred to it as the household of faith. It is a personal reality that deals with the hearts and souls of women and men.

In Ephesians 2:19, the apostle Paul wrote as follows:

> That's plain enough, isn't it? You're no longer wandering exiles. This kingdom of faith is now your home country. You're no longer strangers or outsiders. You *belong* here, with as much right to the name Christian as anyone. God is building a home. He's using us all — irrespective of how we got here — in what he is building.

And again in Colossians 1:13-14:

> God rescued us from dead-end alleys and dark dungeons. He's set us up in the kingdom of the Son he loves so much, the Son who got us out of the pit we were in, got rid of the sins we were doomed to keep repeating.

Q8. What do these verses tell you about being a citizen of God's kingdom?

You Are Family

Paul also described those who follow Christ as being "insiders" or family members. As a family member, you are a member of a new community of brothers and sisters. No longer are you identified based on your physical, ethnic, or religious identity. No matter what you were before, you are now part of a family with rights to all its privileges and responsibilities.

Every culture has its criteria for becoming an "insider." It could be based on looks, language, or city of origin. In Paul's culture, there were two main divisions. The religious Jews were the insiders; the pagan Gentiles, the outsiders. But when Jesus arrived on the scene, He changed the picture. No longer were the Jews the only people who had an "in" with God.

The apostle Paul said in Ephesians 2:11-13:

> But don't take any of this for granted. It was only yesterday that you outsiders to God's ways had no idea of any of this, didn't know the first thing about the way God works, hadn't the faintest idea of Christ. You knew nothing of that rich history of God's covenants and promises in Israel, hadn't a clue about what God was doing in the world at large. Now because of Christ — dying that death, shedding that blood — you who were once out of it altogether are in on everything.

And again in Colossians 1:26-27:

> This mystery has been kept in the dark for a long time, but now it's out in the open. God wanted everyone, not just Jews, to know this rich and glorious secret inside and out, regardless of their background, regardless of their religious standing. The mystery in a nutshell is just this: Christ is in you, therefore you can look forward to sharing in God's glory. It's that simple. That is the substance of our Message.

Q9. What do these passages say about you as a member of God's family?

On a news program, a reporter revealed that millions of dollars of inheritance are locked up in the vaults of city and state governments. Jewelry, stocks, and cash, each clearly identified with the names of the inheritors, remain unclaimed. The reason the treasures remain unclaimed is that the inheritors are unaware of their existence.

The treasure is there, taking up space in a vault and waiting to be claimed. All it takes is for the right people to identify themselves and collect what is legally theirs. As a child of God, you also have an inheritance waiting for you. Paul prayed the following prayer for the new believers in Ephesus:

> I pray that the eyes of your heart may be enlightened, so that you will know what is the hope of His calling, what are the riches of the glory of His inheritance in the saints, and what is the surpassing greatness of His power toward us who believe. These are in accordance with the working of the strength of His might. (Ephesians 1:18-19, NASB)

Living in light of your inheritance is part of the joy of discovery along the journey. Paul wrote in Ephesians 1:3-8:

> How blessed is God! And what a blessing he is! He's the Father of our Master, Jesus Christ, and takes us to the high places of blessing in him. Long before he laid down earth's foundations, he had us in mind, had settled on us as the focus of his love, to be made whole and holy by his love. Long, long ago he decided to adopt us into his family through Jesus Christ. (What pleasure he took in planning this!) He wanted us to enter into the celebration of his lavish gift-giving by the hand of his beloved Son. Because of the sacrifice of the Messiah, his blood poured out on the altar of the Cross, we're a free people — free of penalties and punishments chalked up by all our misdeeds. And not just barely free, either. *Abundantly* free! He thought of everything, provided for everything we could possibly need.

Q10. According to the previous passage, what is your inheritance as a family member?

Q11. What might be the consequences of not knowing about or not claiming your inheritance?

SUMMARY

In Christ you are a brand-new creation. God has changed your essential being. He has not only forgiven you but has also given you a brand-new identity. You are now spiritually alive, a saint, a citizen of God's kingdom, and a rightful member of His family.

PRAYER

Father, I admit that I don't always feel like the person You say I am. I need Your help in changing the way I think about You and myself. It is awesome that You have made me Your child and given me the rights and privileges of a family member. Help me live today in light of my new identity and experience more of its reality in my heart and mind.

New Center

NEXT STEPS

Your journey with Christ takes you into brand-new territory. In order to understand where you are going, it's important to see the big picture. Christ is at the center, and He is the source of everything you will need. Because of His centrality you will have a new perspective on all you do and say.

We look at this Son and see the God who cannot be seen. We look at this Son and see God's original purpose in everything created.
COLOSSIANS 1:15

*P*aul, writing to a group of first-century new believers in the Roman city of Colosse, described the centrality of Christ in the world and in the life of each believer:

> We look at this Son and see the God who cannot be seen. We look at this Son and see God's original purpose in everything created. For everything, absolutely everything, above and below, visible and invisible, rank after rank after rank of angels — *everything* got started in him and finds its purpose in him. He was there before any of it came into existence and holds it all together right up to this moment. And when it comes to the church, he organizes and holds it together, like a head does a body. He was supreme in the beginning and — leading the resurrection parade — he is supreme in the end. From beginning to end he's there, towering far above everything, everyone. (Colossians 1:15-18)

Q1. What does this passage tell you about Jesus?

Q2. What is your initial reaction to what Paul said about Jesus? How does what Paul said impact what you think about Jesus?

The term *church* means "calling out," or an assembly or popular meeting, especially a religious congregation. The word *church* can also refer to believers in Christ no matter where they are; it is not limited by geography. The "body of Christ" metaphor (referenced earlier in Paul's mention of Jesus as the "head") paints a picture of the church that suggests the way the church works (or ought to work).

Today we often use the term *church* to describe a building where Christians go to worship. Yet when the Bible talks about a church, it is referring not to a steeple-topped building but to a group of believers meeting together. There were no church buildings in New Testament times, so believers met in private homes.

Q3. How do these statements regarding the church compare to what you have believed in the past?

CHRIST THE REVEALER OF GOD

The Rosetta Stone is a compact basalt slab that was found in July 1799 in the small Egyptian village of Rosette. It contains three inscriptions that repre-

sent a single text. Its discovery signaled a breakthrough in the research of Egyptian hieroglyphs. The representation of a single text in the three script variants enabled the French scholar Jean François Champollion in 1822 to decipher hieroglyphs, which up to that time were not understood.

Jesus is God's Rosetta Stone. God, only partially understood from reading the Old Testament, is revealed through Jesus in language we understand. He is God in human form, living among us.

Jesus is the revelation of God. By looking at Jesus, we can see God. The Old Testament is not merely a collection of history books, but a revelation of who God is. In the Old Testament, God revealed Himself as He related to specific people and groups of people over hundreds of years. Through reading their stories, we learn something of the nature of God. But the greatest revelation of God came when He entered our space/time world as one of us. Jesus, also called the Christ or Messiah, is God in human form, revealing a true picture of God.

The New Testament book of Hebrews was written to help us understand more of who Jesus is and how He clarifies the events and messages of the Old Testament.

Hebrews 1:1-4 speaks of Jesus as the Son of God:

> In the past God spoke to our forefathers through the prophets at many times and in various ways, but in these last days he has spoken to us by his Son, whom he appointed heir of all things, and through whom he made the universe. The Son is the radiance of God's glory and the exact representation of his being, sustaining all things by his powerful word. After he had provided purification for sins, he sat down at the right hand of the Majesty in heaven. So he became as much superior to the angels as the name he has inherited is superior to theirs. (NIV)

Q4. What does this passage tell you about Jesus?

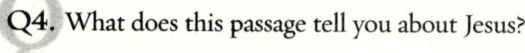

In essence, the writer of Hebrews was saying, "If you want to know what God is like, look at Jesus." Jesus made the same connection when Philip, one of His disciples, asked Jesus to show him the Father (God):

> Philip said, "Master, show us the Father; then we'll be content." [Jesus replied,] "You've been with me all this time, Philip, and you still don't understand? To see me is to see the Father. So how can you ask, 'Where is the Father?'" (John 14:8-9)

The Bible tells us that in order to understand and know God, we must concentrate on knowing and understanding Jesus. The first four books of the New Testament, referred to as the Gospels, are unique accounts of the life and ministry of Jesus. The rest of the New Testament is made up primarily of letters about Jesus written by apostles to first-century believers. Today we not only have the Bible that gives us the historical view, but we also have the Holy Spirit who gives us understanding.

In our culture, people tend to treat the invisible as less real than the visible. Yet with a little reflection, we must admit that much of what is real in our world is invisible. Jesus, no longer physically present, is still present through His Spirit. Jesus told His initial disciples that after His resurrection, His presence would be even greater. His physical presence limited Jesus to a single location at a given time. But after His resurrection, through His Spirit, He is now universally present in all believers, all the time, everywhere.

Q5. How can a person know and relate to Jesus who is present, yet invisible?

Communication with Jesus is possible today. As you read the Bible, God can speak to you. The Bible can show you how to live effectively. It is a personal love letter written by God to each of His children.

You can also communicate with Jesus through prayer. Prayer doesn't require big, fancy words or a specific location or posture. Prayer is simply talking to God by telling Him what you know about Him, expressing your concerns and asking for His help, and thanking Him for His answers.

Take time each day this week to read the Bible and pray. Express to God what you are learning. Through this spiritual dialogue, you will grow a powerful and real relationship with God.

> Jesus, or Jesus of Nazareth, was the common name given to God the Son when He came into human form. Jesus was also given various explanatory titles during His life and ministry. He was called Teacher, Master, or Lord. He claimed to be the Son of God (or Son) and the Jewish Messiah, the promised deliverer of Israel. The term *Christ* is the Greek translation of the Jewish title *Messiah*. Jesus is often referred to in the Bible as Christ or Jesus the Christ. Today we often incorrectly refer to Him as Jesus Christ as though it were a first and last name. Actually, it is a first name and a title.

CHRIST THE LEADER

The Bible teaches that although Christ came quietly into our world as a baby, lived as an obscure teacher in an out-of-the-way nation, died a criminal's cruel death, and was buried in a borrowed grave, He is anything but insignificant.

The Romans considered the title given to Jesus, "King of the Jews," and saw no threat to their control. To them He was a minor irritation, easily dealt with and summarily dismissed. What they failed to see was that this ordinary looking man would build a mighty kingdom that would outlast Rome and every other nation in history. His kingdom would start small, grow until it eclipsed them all, and then, amazingly, last forever.

The Old Testament paints two pictures of the coming Messiah, of Jesus. In one picture, Jesus is painted as a king. In the other, He is painted as a servant. The first-century Jews fully expected their Messiah to come into the world as a king — to take charge, rid them of the oppressive rule of Rome, and set them politically free. Jesus of Nazareth was a disappointment to them. He led no revolution against Roman rule but instead taught about God and a kingdom that seemed strangely vague.

Paul wrote the following in Ephesians 1:20-23:

All this energy issues from Christ: God raised him from death and set him on a throne in deep heaven, in charge of running the universe, everything from galaxies to governments, no name and no power exempt from his rule. And not just for the time being, but *forever*. He is in charge of it all, has the final word on everything. At the center of all this, Christ rules the church. The church, you see, is not peripheral to the world; the world is peripheral to the church.

Q6. What does this passage say is true about Jesus?

Jesus came into our world initially as a suffering servant. He will come again as a conquering king. The final book of the New Testament records visions God gave the apostle John about the future. Many are difficult to understand, but one that is fairly clear portrays Jesus as the triumphant King:

Then I saw Heaven open wide — and oh! a white horse and its Rider. The Rider, named Faithful and True, judges and makes war in pure righteousness. His eyes are a blaze of fire, on his head many crowns. He has a Name inscribed that's known only to himself. He is dressed in a robe soaked with blood, and he is addressed as "Word of God." The armies of Heaven, mounted on white horses and dressed in dazzling white linen, follow him. A sharp sword comes out of his mouth so he can subdue the nations, then rule them with a rod of iron. He treads the winepress of the raging wrath of God, the Sovereign-Strong. On his robe and thigh is written, KING OF KINGS, LORD OF LORDS. (Revelation 19:11-16)

Q7. As you read this passage, what do you see? How does it make you feel?

Q8. What are the possible responses people might have to Jesus' return as a king?

It may not appear at this moment that Jesus is in control of the world and its events. Yet the Bible teaches that nothing that happens today or tomorrow is outside the loving authority of Christ. Today Christ rules unseen, visible only to those who have placed themselves in faith under His authority. Someday, His authority will be visible to all.

SUMMARY

Christ is the focus of history. Everything finds its fulfillment in Him. He is the source and sustainer of life. Our journey finds its meaning, purpose, and destination in Him. Christ is the center around which we find our place, the explanation of the invisible God, and the gracious leader for those who choose to follow Him.

PRAYER

Thank You, Lord, for giving me a new center for my life. I need You as my anchor, my foundation, my compass. I have a tendency to drift in the wind, to drift off course under the pressures of daily living. I thank You for Your presence and patience to guide my journey through the uncharted waters ahead. Help me keep my eyes on You rather than on the circumstances that come my way.

New Companionship

NEXT STEPS

You are not alone as you travel this journey. God goes before you, He walks beside you, and He lives within you. Nothing can separate you from Him. The journey involves learning to recognize His companionship and loving presence.

God can do anything, you know—far more than you could ever imagine or guess or request in your wildest dreams! He does it not by pushing us around but by working within us, his Spirit deeply and gently within us.
EPHESIANS 3:20

To understand the awesome reality of having the God of the universe as your companion on this journey will require a look at three aspects of His companionship. First is the reality that God is not against you, but for you. He is on your side. Second, God is with you, coming alongside you as your constant companion, guide, and coach. He knows the route, the hazards, and the beautiful vistas you'll encounter along the way. His promise to be with you is one of the most repeated concepts in Scripture. Third, God is actually *in* you by His Spirit, bringing an intimacy that is closer than anything you have ever known.

HE IS FOR US
In Luke 15:11-32, we find one of the most familiar stories in the Bible, a story Rembrandt captured in his classic painting *The Return of the Prodigal Son.* Among the story's many lessons is the persistent love of the father. The story begins like this:

> "There was once a man who had two sons. The younger said to his father, 'Father, I want right now what's coming to me.'

> "So the father divided the property between them. It wasn't long before the younger son packed his bags and left for a distant country. There, undisciplined and dissipated, he wasted everything he had." (verses 11-13)

Q1. What might have motivated the son to claim his inheritance and leave home?

The story continues:

> "After he had gone through all his money, there was a bad famine all through that country and he began to hurt. He signed on with a citizen there who assigned him to his fields to slop the pigs. He was so hungry he would have eaten the corncobs in the pig slop, but no one would give him any.
>
> "That brought him to his senses. He said, 'All those farmhands working for my father sit down to three meals a day, and here I am starving to death. I'm going back to my father. I'll say to him, Father, I've sinned against God, I've sinned before you; I don't deserve to be called your son. Take me on as a hired hand.'" (verses 14-19)

Q2. What changes occurred in the son during this part of the story?

Jesus concluded the story with His point about unconditional love:

> "He got right up and went home to his father.
> "When he was still a long way off, his father saw him. His

heart pounding, he ran out, embraced him, and kissed him. The son started his speech: 'Father, I've sinned against God, I've sinned before you; I don't deserve to be called your son ever again.'

"But the father wasn't listening. He was calling to the servants, 'Quick. Bring a clean set of clothes and dress him. Put the family ring on his finger and sandals on his feet. Then get a grain-fed heifer and roast it. We're going to feast! We're going to have a wonderful time! My son is here — given up for dead and now alive! Given up for lost and now found!' And they began to have a wonderful time.

"All this time his older son was out in the field. When the day's work was done he came in. As he approached the house, he heard the music and dancing. Calling over one of the houseboys, he asked what was going on. He told him, 'Your brother came home. Your father has ordered a feast — barbecued beef!—because he has him home safe and sound.'

"The older brother stalked off in an angry sulk and refused to join in. His father came out and tried to talk to him, but he wouldn't listen. The son said, 'Look how many years I've stayed here serving you, never giving you one moment of grief, but have you ever thrown a party for me and my friends? Then this son of yours who has thrown away your money on whores shows up and you go all out with a feast!'

"His father said, 'Son, you don't understand. You're with me all the time, and everything that is mine is yours — but this is a wonderful time, and we had to celebrate. This brother of yours was dead, and he's alive! He was lost, and he's found!'"

Q3. If you had been the father, how would you have reacted? How did the father act? Why?

Q4. Compare the response of the elder brother to that of the father.

This story helps us see God's persistent love for His children. People often come to faith in Christ and find forgiveness from their past sin but secretly doubt if God is really *for* them. They believe He accepts them but can't imagine He would want to throw them a party. They wonder if there is a hidden catch. They wonder if God is waiting to see if they will really prove their merit or sincerity. They wonder if perhaps they need to work off some of the debt. The idea that God is throwing an extravagant party just for them — just because they came home — is humbling and hard to believe. In Romans 8:31,38-39, Paul expressed it this way:

> What then shall we say to these things? If God is for us, who is against us? . . . For I am convinced that neither death, nor life, nor angels, nor principalities, nor things present, nor things to come, nor powers, nor height, nor depth, nor any other created thing, will be able to separate us from the love of God, which is in Christ Jesus our Lord. (NASB)

Q5. What thoughts or beliefs make it difficult for you to experience God's love?

Q6. If you really believed that nothing could separate you from God's love, how would you live your life?

Satan will tempt you to doubt that God is on your side. He will remind you of failures, weaknesses, inconsistencies, and unkept promises. He wants you to doubt the love of God and God's faithfulness to you. When those thoughts enter your mind, review this great truth: Personal faith in Christ guarantees God's total acceptance. God is now for you as He is for Christ Himself. You travel this journey with God as your champion and companion.

HE IS WITH US

When our youngest son was about four, we built a home on a few acres that had a pond and some timber. One evening as the sun was going down, I asked him if he would like to go for a walk in the woods. With the enthusiasm common to that age, he ran ahead of me until we crossed the dam and approached the edge of the woods. As we approached the tree line, he dropped back and only reluctantly followed me.

I leaned down and asked, "Son, are you afraid?" He nodded his head immediately. "What are you afraid of?" He thought for a moment and said, "The bears!"

I knew it was irrelevant at that moment to inform him that there had not been a bear in these woods in over two hundred years. But I did reach down and take his hand in mine. The transformation was immediate. Reluctance was replaced by enthusiasm, fear was replaced by courage, and silence was replaced by laughter. The difference was the assurance of my presence.

Along our faith journey, we will face the real and imaginary "bears" of life. Knowing that God has reached down and taken our hand can mean the difference between fear and peace, between hesitancy and courage.

At the very beginning of the New Testament when God announced the birth of Christ, He called Him Emmanuel, which means "God with us." And when Christ was about to leave His disciples after His resurrection, He gave them instructions that ended with a promise:

> "Go out and train everyone you meet, far and near, in this way of life, marking them by baptism in the threefold name: Father, Son, and Holy Spirit. Then instruct them in the practice of all I have commanded you. I'll be with you as you do this, day after day after day, right up to the end of the age." (Matthew 28:19-20)

Q7. What is the promise in this passage?

Q8. Describe an experience in your life when someone's presence made a difference. How does it feel to know that God is always with you?

He Is in Us

While it is relatively easy to understand that God is for us and beside us, the amazing concept that God is also in us is a little more difficult to comprehend. Paul wrote in Colossians 1:26-27:

> This mystery has been kept in the dark for a long time, but now it's out in the open. God wanted everyone, not just Jews, to know this rich and glorious secret inside and out, regardless of their background, regardless of their religious standing. The mystery in a nutshell is just this: Christ is in you, therefore you can look forward to sharing in God's glory. It's that simple. That is the substance of our Message.

In the Old Testament times, God's presence was confined to a building or structure (called the tabernacle or temple). Those serious about worshiping God could go there to meet with and experience the presence of God.

In the period of history covered by the New Testament Gospels (the first four books), God was present in Christ. Yet Christ was limited in space by a physical body. Amazing as His life was during His thirty-plus years on earth, only a few people experienced His presence. His whole life was confined to the geography of modern-day Israel.

The week before His crucifixion and resurrection, Jesus told His disciples that He was going away but that He would send His Spirit to live in them. The book of Acts in the New Testament records some of the dramatic changes that took place when His Spirit took up residence in the lives of believers.

The apostle Paul put it this way in 1 Corinthians 3:16: "You realize, don't you, that you are the temple of God, and God himself is present in you?" He explained it further in Ephesians 1:13-14:

> And now you also have heard the truth, the Good News that God saves you. And when you believed in Christ, he identified you as his own by giving you the Holy Spirit, whom he promised long ago. The Spirit is God's guarantee that he will give us everything he promised and that he has purchased us to be his own people. This is just one more reason for us to praise our glorious God. (NLT)

Q9. According to this passage, what are the results of being given the Holy Spirit?

Because we now have His Spirit within us, we don't have to go to a particular place to experience God's presence. His presence is dramatically exposed in the lives of every follower of Christ. We are in fact little temples — each one of us a center of worship and divine presence.

Q10. Summarize what you have learned about God being:

• For you

• With you

• In you

SUMMARY

Christ is now our constant companion. He goes before us, walks beside us, and lives within us. He knows the path, the destination, and all the hazards ahead. He is our constant defender and promoter. He is for us, with us, and in us.

PRAYER

Thank You, Lord, for being my greatest fan. Your love for me is beyond my comprehension. Your presence with me is my comfort and joy. I know that You will never leave, abandon, or desert me. There is no place I can go where You will not guide and comfort me. Thank You for sending Your Spirit to live and dwell in my life, turning my humble body into a temple of God.

New Clothes

NEXT STEPS

As we continue on our journey, God's plan is to change us to be like Christ. This change includes putting on a new wardrobe that reflects who we are in Christ. But before we put on new clothes, we must take off the old.

> *Now you're dressed in a new wardrobe. Every item of your new way of life is custom-made by the Creator, with his label on it. All the old fashions are now obsolete.*
>
> COLOSSIANS 3:10

While attending a conference at Calloway Gardens in Georgia a few years ago, we took a walking tour through a large tropical environment where butterflies were raised. The brilliant colors of the numerous butterflies were a sensory delight. It is hard to imagine that such beauty began as fuzzy, dull caterpillars. Yet through the process of metamorphosis, caterpillars become butterflies. One form is exchanged for another.

Just like a caterpillar changes to a butterfly, God is in the process of changing us from the inside out — exchanging old values for new and replacing old habits, motives, behavior, and character. We are being changed into the image of Christ, one day at a time.

NEW IMAGE
Once the Spirit of God comes into our lives, a change or metamorphosis begins. God's power begins to work within our hearts and minds to transform us into the image and nature of Christ. We begin to take on the family image with Christ as our model.

Jesus said in Luke 6:40, "A pupil is not above his teacher; but everyone, after he has been fully trained, will be like his teacher" (NASB). When Christ is our teacher, we will become like Him. Paul put it this way in 2 Corinthians 3:18: "All of us have had that veil removed so that we can be mirrors that brightly reflect the glory of the Lord. And as the Spirit of the Lord works within us, we become more and more like him and reflect his glory even more" (NLT).

Q1. What is the image that God is perfecting in us?

Initially, Christ's followers were called "disciples." But as the message spread into the Roman Empire, Christ's followers were called "followers of The Way" and eventually "Christians," which meant "Christ-like ones." Today, the term *Christian* has lost much of that original meaning. But God's purpose remains the same: to develop a people who reflect the nature and image of His Son. While we each maintain our unique personality, we are expected to exhibit the character, values, and beliefs of Christ in our daily lives and interactions with other people.

CHANGED INSIDE AND OUT

Because Jesus is the exact representation of God, when we observe His life in the Gospels, we see not only what God is like but also what *we* are to be like. In Ephesians 4:22-24, Paul stated:

> Since, then, we do not have the excuse of ignorance, every-thing — and I do mean everything — connected with that old way of life has to go. It's rotten through and through. Get rid of it! And then take on an entirely new way of life — a God-fashioned life, a life renewed from the inside and working itself into your conduct as God accurately reproduces his character in you.

Q2. What do these verses say about how you are to relate to your old way of life?

Although changing our behavior can be beneficial in and of itself, it can still leave our hearts untouched. Throughout my life, as I became aware of anger's detrimental effect on various relationships, I learned helpful techniques to control my anger. I learned to avoid those things that triggered angry outbursts. I mastered techniques to control the expression of my anger at critical moments. But I would still get angry. I saw that behavior modification was not enough.

A key part of inside-out change is the work of the Holy Spirit. Paul referred to this in Galatians 5:22-23 as follows: "But when the Holy Spirit controls our lives, he will produce this kind of fruit in us: love, joy, peace, patience, kindness, goodness, faithfulness, gentleness, and self control" (NLT).

Q3. What does it mean that the Holy Spirit "controls our lives"?

Inside-out change also involves cooperation with the Holy Spirit. Paul said in Romans 12:1-2:

> So here's what I want you to do, God helping you: Take your everyday, ordinary life — your sleeping, eating, going-to-work, and walking-around life — and place it before God as an offering. Embracing what God does for you is the best thing you can do for him. Don't become so well-adjusted to your culture that you fit into it without even thinking. Instead, fix your attention on God. You'll be changed from the inside out. Readily recognize what he wants from you, and quickly

> respond to it. Unlike the culture around you, always dragging you down to its level of immaturity, God brings the best out of you, develops well-formed maturity in you.

Q4. Based on this passage, what does God desire to do in you? What is your role?

God wanted to bring about real change in my life that was much deeper than simply controlling my anger. He desires change that touches our values, beliefs, and character, as well as our actions. As I prayed about this, I also began to memorize verses from the Bible that gave God's perspective on anger. The Holy Spirit took those truths and began to place them in my mind and heart to make me more patient on the inside and less angry on the outside. Real change began to take place. As we cooperate with God's Spirit within us, we become more of a true reflection of Christ. Real change happens from the inside out.

This change takes time, understanding, faith, and obedience. Like a gardener, we don't control the growth process, but we can make sure we have the right mix of water, soil, and sun. Allowing your mind to soak up the truth of Scripture is like letting a plant soak up the nutrients it needs to be healthy.

God wants this inner change or transformation to be comprehensive — affecting our minds, hearts, and wills. He wants to bring your will and emotions in line with His nature. As you cooperate with His Spirit, God powerfully changes you from the inside out.

Memorizing Scripture can help you change from the inside out. Start by memorizing the theme verse for this series: "Therefore as you have received Christ Jesus the Lord, so walk in Him" (Colossians 2:6, NASB).

Write the key verse for each lesson on a 3 x 5 card. Carry the cards with you and review the verses a few times each day. You will be surprised how easy it is to remember the verses. Memorizing Scripture is a classic and historic method for walking with Christ.

WHAT TO REMOVE

If we are to "dress for success," we first need to get rid of our old clothes that are ill-fitting, out of style, ragged, and worn out. Our old way of life represents behaviors and values that are ill-fitting for kingdom living. In Colossians 3:5-8, Paul identified some of the "old clothes" that need to be removed:

> And that means killing off everything connected with that way of death: sexual promiscuity, impurity, lust, doing whatever you feel like whenever you feel like it, and grabbing whatever attracts your fancy. That's a life shaped by things and feelings instead of by God. It's because of this kind of thing that God is about to explode in anger. It wasn't long ago that you were doing all that stuff and not knowing any better. But you know better now, so make sure it's all gone for good: bad temper, irritability, meanness, profanity, dirty talk.

Q5. What old clothes do you need to remove?

WHAT TO PUT ON

Getting rid of those old clothes is often difficult and takes time. But the effort is worthwhile because the wardrobe God has for you is designer quality and appropriate for your journey. The longer you walk with Christ, the better the new clothes fit and feel. Paul said in Colossians 3:9-14:

> Don't lie to one another. You're done with that old life. It's like a filthy set of ill-fitting clothes you've stripped off and put in the fire. Now you're dressed in a new wardrobe. Every item of your new way of life is custom-made by the Creator, with his label on it. All the old fashions are now obsolete. Words like Jewish and non-Jewish, religious and irreligious,

insider and outsider, uncivilized and uncouth, slave and free, mean nothing. From now on everyone is defined by Christ, everyone is included in Christ. So, chosen by God for this new life of love, dress in the wardrobe God picked out for you: compassion, kindness, humility, quiet strength, discipline. Be even-tempered, content with second place, quick to forgive an offense. Forgive as quickly and completely as the Master forgave you. And regardless of what else you put on, wear love. It's your basic, all-purpose garment. Never be without it.

Q6. List three items included in this passage that you will use to make up your new wardrobe.

Q7. What is the one basic "garment" that fits you for the journey, regardless of the weather or terrain?

Q8. Why is love fundamental to any outfit you might choose?

From gang members in the inner city to businesspeople on Wall Street, people are identified or judged (right or wrong) by the clothes they wear. In John 13:34-35, Jesus told His disciples that the world would judge how close they were to Him based on how well they were clothed with love toward one another. He said, "Let me give you a new command: Love one another. In the same way I loved you, you love one another. This is how everyone will recognize that you are my disciples — when they see the love you have for each other."

The most distinctive mark of a Christ-follower is how he or she expresses love. Sacrificial love gives while demanding nothing in return. This is the kind of love Jesus demonstrates toward us and the kind we are to show to one another.

SUMMARY

As we travel the journey with Christ, we will become like Him. We will reflect His nature and character. God has a new wardrobe for us to put on that reflects our new nature. It involves both taking off our old habits and patterns of behavior and putting on new ones. It is more than just behavior modification, however. It is a change from the inside out.

PRAYER

Lord, change me today to look more like You. Replace the discord of my heart with the melody of Your Spirit. May my life today touch others with the reality of Your love. Change me by Your power so that the only possible explanation of who I am becoming is the touch of Your presence.

New Calling

NEXT STEPS

God has called us to experience an awesome life. He invites us to join Him in accomplishing His purposes. Life is not meager, dull, or boring when we follow Christ. He is doing something big and wants us to be a part. Knowing and participating in what God is doing will make your journey significant.

> *You were all called to travel on the same road and in the same direction,*
> *so stay together, both outwardly and inwardly.*
> EPHESIANS 4:4

On a trip to China, I stopped in a factory where artisans were weaving silk rugs by hand on wooden looms. The weaver was constantly adding new yarn as the color and pattern changed. Looking over the weaver's shoulder, the rug was unimpressive. Knots were prominent, and the pattern was obscured. But when I walked around the loom and saw the rug from the other side, its beauty was obvious. It is now hanging on a wall in our living room!

God is the divine artisan who is weaving our life story into a beautiful pattern. From one side we see the knots and scars, but God is able to take each experience and fashion a work of art.

Coming to faith in Christ brings with it a new start and a new direction. We are no longer left to wander aimlessly. Christ has called us on a path of purpose. His plan for us began before the world was created.

The word *calling* means a mission, work, or vocation. The Bible teaches that man, created in the image of God, has a mission. Through Christ we can discover our mission and join Him in accomplishing it. In the Old Testament, God reminded His family of their call to an extraordinary life.

This is what He said in Jeremiah 29:11: "I know what I'm doing. I have it all planned out — plans to take care of you, not abandon you, plans to give you the future you hope for." Jesus expressed the same idea in the New Testament in John 10:10: "I came so they can have real and eternal life, more and better life than they ever dreamed of."

God wants us to know where we are going. He has given us all an outline of what our journey will involve. The details of His plan will be filled in as we go along, but our calling from God is clear. As you understand and participate in His calling, you will enjoy tastes of the abundant life Jesus promised. The apostle Paul was so convinced of this that it became part of his prayer for the new believers in Ephesus. In Ephesians 1:17-18 he said, "I ask — ask the God of our Master, Jesus Christ, the God of glory — to make you intelligent and discerning in knowing him personally, your eyes focused and clear, so that you can see exactly what it is he is calling you to do, grasp the immensity of this glorious way of life he has for Christians."

CALLED TO EXPERIENCE GOD'S DIVINE LOVE

Paul began his letter to the new believers in Ephesus by reminding them that, from the beginning, God has made us the center of His love. In Ephesians 1:4, he said, "Long before he laid down earth's foundations, he had us in mind, had settled on us as the focus of his love."

God wants to touch people with His incredible love. God wants us to know from deep, personal experience that He loves us with a love that is beyond our wildest imagination. Paul's prayer for the new believers in Ephesus included a plea to seek out that kind of love:

> I ask him to strengthen you by his Spirit — not a brute strength but a glorious inner strength — that Christ will live in you as you open the door and invite him in. And I ask him that with both feet planted firmly on love, you'll be able to take in with all Christians the extravagant dimensions of Christ's love. Reach out and experience the breadth! Test its length! Plumb the depths! Rise to the heights! Live full lives, full in the fullness of God. (Ephesians 3:16-19)

Q1. Write this prayer in your own words.

Knowing something as a fact or experiencing it as a personal reality can be worlds apart. You probably have seen pictures of the earth taken from inside one of NASA's shuttles. You may have heard the astronauts' excitement as they attempted to explain what it's like to look at our planet from hundreds of miles away in space. Yet no explanation or picture can substitute for actually being there. We can know *about* it, but the astronauts know by experience.

In the same way, you can read about God's love, hear it described, and even know people who have experienced it. You can believe that God loves you without experiencing it personally. God wants you to know His love not simply by looking at Him, but by being closely involved with Him. Take a look at what Ephesians 5:1-2 says:

> Watch what God does, and then you do it, like children who learn proper behavior from their parents. Mostly what God does is love you. Keep company with him and learn a life of love. Observe how Christ loved us. His love was not cautious but extravagant. He didn't love in order to get something from us but to give everything of himself to us. Love like that.

Q2. What do these verses say to you about God's love?

Q3. What is your response to God's love?

CALLED TO PERSONAL SPIRITUAL MATURITY

God desires followers who are holy, mature, and strong in their life of faith. But we don't start out that way. Spiritual maturity is a matter of time and of understanding God's Word and obeying it.

Paul said we begin our faith journey as infants and grow into maturity. He used this familiar metaphor to help us understand the process that God is taking us through. Even as young children, we think and act in a way that is appropriate for our age. But as we mature, we learn to act differently. Each stage of development along the way is critical.

Maturity in our spiritual journey results from three things:

1. Understanding God's Word
2. Applying God's truth to our lives
3. Growing over time

Reading the Bible is an important part of the growth process for a new follower of Christ. The apostle Peter wrote in 1 Peter 2:2, "Like newborn babies, long for the pure milk of the word, so that by it you may grow in respect to salvation" (NASB). And Jesus said in Matthew 4:4, "It is written, 'MAN SHALL NOT LIVE ON BREAD ALONE, BUT ON EVERY WORD THAT PROCEEDS OUT OF THE MOUTH OF GOD'" (NASB).

DEEPENING YOUR WALK

Obtain a modern translation or paraphrase of the New Testament and read it as God's personal letter to you. As you read, ask yourself the following questions:

• What does what I read tell me about God?
• What does what I read imply about me?
• What changes should I consider based on what I am learning about God or myself?

Paul stated the following in Ephesians 4:12-15:

> [God enables leaders] to train Christians in skilled servant work, working within Christ's body, the church, until we're all moving rhythmically and easily with each other, efficient and graceful in response to God's Son, fully mature adults, fully developed within and without, fully alive like Christ. No prolonged infancies among us, please. We'll not tolerate babes in the woods, small children who are an easy mark for impostors. God wants us to grow up, to know the whole truth and tell it in love — like Christ in everything. We take our lead from Christ, who is the source of everything we do.

Q4. How do these verses describe adults who are mature in faith?

Q5. What do the verses say about those who remain infants in their faith?

Note: For more information on the resources that can help grow your faith, consider getting a copy of another book in this series: *Jesus: The Life*.

CALLED TO AUTHENTIC COMMUNITY WITH OTHERS

God is building a community of faith where all people belong, regardless of their past. There are no divisions or special classes in this community. Regardless of what or who we were, where we have come from, or how we got here, the ground is level for us who are in Christ. Paul made this point very clear in Ephesians 2:18-20:

> He treated us as equals, and so made us equals. Through him we both share the same Spirit and have equal access to the Father. That's plain enough, isn't it? You're no longer wandering exiles. This kingdom of faith is now your home country. You're no longer strangers or outsiders. You *belong* here, with as much right to the name Christian as anyone. God is building a home. He's using us all — irrespective of how we got here — in what he is building. He used the apostles and prophets for the foundation. Now he's using you, fitting you in brick by brick, stone by stone, with Christ Jesus as the cornerstone.

Q6. What do these verses say is true about each person who has come to Christ by faith?

The community of faith is a place where everyone is welcome and accepted. It's a family that crosses ethnic and social boundaries. God's design for this community, called the church, is to create a place where everyone involved experiences mutual acceptance and harmony.

As part of God's family, we each have a contribution to make to the lives of others. Our relationship with Christ will naturally overflow into loving service to others. Paul wrote in Ephesians 2:10, "No, we neither make nor save ourselves. God does both the making and saving. He creates each of us by Christ Jesus to join him in the work he does, the good work he has gotten ready for us to do, work we had better be doing."

Q7. What do you think Paul had in mind when he referred to "the work he does"?

Community is experienced not only in large group settings, usually called worship or celebration services, but also in small groups and mentoring relationships. As you begin your journey, seek out a variety of ways to experience this community.

You are a significant and essential part of God's community. Because you are unique, no one can take your place. The more you live and learn on your journey, the more you will discover where you fit within the community of Christ.

Q8. Where can you go to find a community for worship and teaching?

Q9. Who might be a good mentor for you as you begin your faith journey? How will you approach this person to see if you might work together?

SUMMARY

We are created and called to God's purposes. His plans go beyond this life into eternity. We are made by God and for God. God has called us to know His love deeply, to grow toward maturity personally, to live in community authentically, and to contribute to others significantly.

PRAYER

Nothing compares to finding my ultimate purpose in You, God. Help me lay aside my trivial pursuits and catch hold of Your grand plan. Help me align my life with the eternal design that is at work and that will ultimately fill the universe. Take my best attempt at finger painting and create a work of art on the canvas of human lives that You allow me to touch. Let Your joy fill my heart as You produce spiritual fruit in and through me.

Summary

*U*se the following chart to review the lessons you have just completed. You may want to show someone else what you have been learning about your journey with Christ.

LESSON	KEY QUESTION	KEY VERSE	KEY CONCEPTS
New Connection 1	Is my relationship with God really different?	Ephesians 2:7	**Because of Christ I am** • Loved by the Father • Freed by the Son • Certified by the Spirit
New Creation 2	Who am I?	2 Corinthians 5:17	**In Christ I am** • Alive • A saint • Forgiven • A citizen of God's kingdom • A member of God's family
New Center 3	Who's in control?	Colossians 1:15	**Christ is** • The center of my world • The revelation of God • The leader of my life
New Companionship 4	Who is walking with me on this journey?	Ephesians 3:20	**Christ is** • For me • With me • In me
New Clothes 5	What attitudes and actions should I "wear"?	Colossians 3:10	**Christ is creating in me** • The family image • An inside-out change • An appropriate wardrobe
New Calling 6	Where am I going?	Ephesians 4:4	**Christ calls me to experience** • Divine love • Spiritual maturity • Authentic community • Personal contribution

Beginning Your Walk

*A*s you consider your journey with Christ, it is important to understand how a relationship with Christ is established.

1. GOD'S PURPOSE

The Bible begins by showing us that God **US** ▬▬▬▬▬▬▬ **GOD** created man (men and women) to share His image and an intimate relationship with Him. Man and woman were in perfect union with God. However, that union was broken by their decision to become morally independent from God. That independence is also called disobedience or sin.

Sin resulted in alienation or separation from God. The intimacy was gone. People and God no longer experienced a personal relationship. People became spiritually dead. That condition has been passed down through every generation since Adam and Eve.

2. OUR PROBLEM

The Bible describes humanity's problem in a statement found in Romans 5:12:

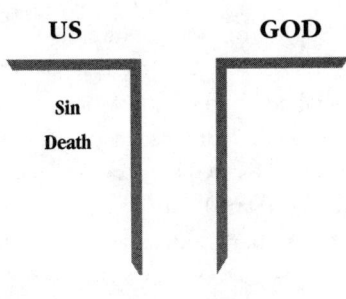

> "You know the story of how Adam landed us in the dilemma we're in — first sin, then death, and no one exempt from either sin or death. That sin disturbed relations with God in everything and everyone."

Death can also be described as separation. Death in its various forms resulted from people's sin and is experienced in every area of life: physical, emotional, social, psychological, and spiritual. Ultimately, death leads to an eternal separation from God and His purpose.

3. GOD'S PLAN

The Bible also reveals God's plan. Read this statement from John 3:16:

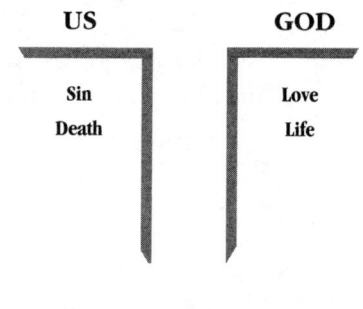

> "This is how much God loved the world: He gave his Son, his one and only Son. And this is why: so that no one need be destroyed; by believing in him, anyone can have a whole and lasting life."

God desires to reestablish the intimacy that was lost and give us life that is eternal.

4. GOD'S PROVISION

Throughout human history people have tried to reach God, primarily through good works. Yet our good works are always inadequate to span the gulf created by sin. Self-effort in any form falls short of God's standard for holiness. His holiness demands that our sin be accounted for, and His love demands a response of grace. God's answer to this

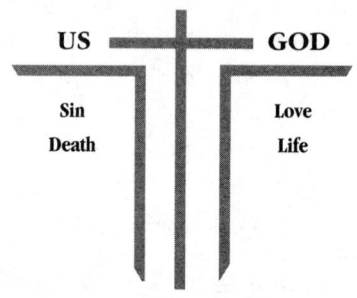

dilemma was to put His love on the line for us by offering His Son in sacrificial death to pay the price for our sin.

Read Romans 5:8 to see how this provision works: "But God demonstrates His own love toward us, in that while we were yet sinners, Christ died for us" (NASB). Notice the progression as it follows the verse: God — loves — us — sinners — Christ — died — for us.

Jesus was God's provision for the problem of our sin. His death and resurrection provided the bridge that can reunite us with God. It is the *only* means by which this union can be restored. Jesus said, "I am the way, and the truth, and the life; no one comes to the Father but through Me" (John 14:6, NASB).

5. Our Privilege

The statement in John 5:24 explains how an individual can cross over the bridge that Christ has provided. Jesus said,

> "Truly, truly, I say to you, he who hears My word, and believes Him who sent Me, has eternal life, and does not come into judgment, but has passed out of death into life" (NASB).

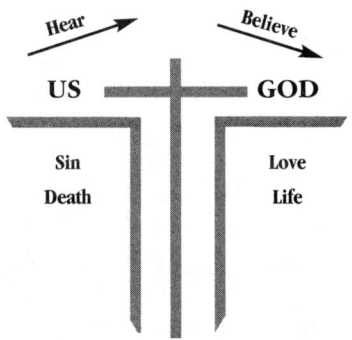

From this statement, notice what Christ is offering us:
1. Eternal life
2. No judgment
3. Passage from death to life

Notice what is necessary to receive this offer:
1. Hear His word
2. Believe in Him (the Father) who sent Christ

The term *belief* means more than acknowledgment of facts or information. "Believe in" means to trust in, commit to, rely upon, or receive. We become children of God and are reunited to a personal relationship with Him when we make a personal commitment of faith. God's provision has been extended to us. It is a gift. And as a gift, we cannot work for it; we can only receive it.

Have you personally put your faith in Jesus Christ as your way to God? If not, would you be willing by faith to accept Christ as your bridge to God right now? You can express this step of faith in a simple prayer in which you tell God:
1. I recognize that I am separate from You as a result of my sin.
2. I recognize that Christ was Your provision for me—that He died for my sin.
3. I want to accept by faith Your gift of forgiveness through Christ.
4. I thank You for Your forgiveness and for accepting me as part of Your family.

About the Authors

Ron and Mary Bennett joined the staff of The Navigators in 1970. They have led ministries on college campuses, in the military, and in the community. They are currently part of the national leadership team of the Church Discipleship Ministry (CDM) within The Navigators. Ron serves as director of the Strategic Resource Group for CDM. He is the author of *Intentional Disciplemaking* and a coauthor of *Opening the Door* and *The Adventure of Discipling Others.*

The *Beginning the Walk* studies were developed by The Navigators' Church Discipleship Ministry (CDM). CDM serves local churches by helping them develop into intentional disciplemaking communities. This series is part of a group of resources that can help equip your church to make disciples. For more information on The Navigators' Church Discipleship Ministry resources, go to www.navigators.org/cdm.

MEET JESUS! THE WAY, THE TRUTH, THE LIFE.

Jesus: The Life
The Navigators
1-57683-708-4

Jesus: The Truth
The Navigators
1-57683-707-6

New from the Church Discipleship Ministry team at The Navigators comes a new Bible study series on the life and supremacy of Jesus Christ.

An excellent resource for new and growing believers, NavPress's BEGINNING THE WALK series focuses on readers' fundamental relationship with Jesus rather than technical details of how to study or interpret the Bible. Participants don't need an extensive church or religious background to get started; mature believers and small-group leaders will find these short, easy-to-use studies the perfect launching pad for intentional discipleship.

To order copies, visit your local Christian bookstore,
call NavPress at 1-800-366-7788,
or log on to www.navpress.com.

To locate a Christian bookstore near you, call 1-800-991-7747.

CHURCH DISCIPLESHIP MINISTRY

CDM is a ministry of The Navigators that focuses on helping churches become more intentional in discipleship and outreach. CDM staff help pastors and church leaders develop an effective and personalized approach to accomplishing the Great Commission.

Through a nationwide network of staff, CDM works alongside the local church to build a strong structure for disciplemaking—one that is intentional. Six critical areas are core to an Intentional Disciplemaking Church:

- Mission

- Spiritual Maturity

- Outreach

- Leadership

- Small Groups

- Life-to-Life

CDM offers seminars, materials, and coaching in these six areas for those interested in becoming an Intentional Disciplemaking Church. See our web page for further information on how CDM can help you.

www.navigators.org/cdm

or call our CDM Office at (719) 598-1212
or write to PO Box 6000, Colorado Springs, CO 80934